Ajata

Robert Wolfe

Karina Library Press
2022

Ajata
by Robert Wolfe

ISBN: 978-1-937902-39-1 paperback

Library of Congress LCCN: 2022949914

Editor
Charles Birns

Karina Library Press
Michael Lommel, publisher
PO Box 35
Ojai, California
93024
www.karinalibrary.com

Author photo, cover: Katherine Holden

This is definitely not a book to reinforce your ideas of who you think you are. If anything, it is about who you aren't, to the ultimate degree. It is about how one lives one's life, despite the fact that we don't, in reality, have one.

from the preface to *Emptiness*
by Robert Wolfe

Robert Wolfe

Emptiness

Living Nonduality

Abiding in Nondual Awareness

Awakening to Infinite Presence

Always—Only—One

Ramana Maharshi: The Teachings of Self-realization

One Essence

Science of the Sages

The Enlightenment Teachings of Jesus

Elementary Cloudwatching

www.ajatasunyata.com

www.livingnonduality.org

Preface

For those who have read *Emptiness*, my previous treatise on the ultimate condition, the book in your hands, *Ajata*, is a deeper dive into the subject.

For those who haven't contemplated this subject, which can turn your perspective of "life" and "death" utterly inside-out, the 33 monographs here were each written to stand alone.

A few of these writings were originally published on my website ajatasunyata.com.

— RW

In considering the relationship between the finite and the infinite, we are led to observe that the whole field of the finite is inherently limited, in that it has no independent existence... We can see this dependent nature of the finite from the fact that every finite thing is transient...

But if the finite has no independent existence, it cannot be all that is.

Physicist David Bohm

The Nondual Teaching

Whenever we speak of "duality", we are indicating two or more things; multiplicity. Each item that we thus refer to is limited to its separate form, whether it is a material object or immaterial, such as an idea. Every separate item stands in relationship to every other item, and so multiple items are also called "relative" items. For example, the word–form "uncle" has no meaning apart from "nephew" or "niece". And "good" is good because it is not "bad".

What is meant when the word "*non*duality" is used? It would refer to that which is "not relative," not limited to any separate form. That which is unlimited in space, we would say is infinite. That which is unlimited in time, we would call eternal. The words infinite and eternal are meant to say "without a beginning or ending".

That which does not begin somewhere or end somewhere in time or in space would be form-less, without any limitations. This is how it is said to be already present everywhere; it is always unbounded, unrestrained.

The dictionary provides a word for such a condition, "Absolute", which means "not relative" and "without limitation". Forms *are* relative and limited, finite. Thus, anything which is finite must exist within the condition of infinity; in other words, all that is relative must be contained within the singular absolute. Yet, at the same time, that which is considered to be absolute must not only surround all that is relative, but it must penetrate and permeate the relative — being unrestricted, unrestrained. It is like, for example, gravity: we know it exists outside of a building, but we know also that it exists inside a building. So this formless presence is not only exterior to everything, but interior as well. Thus, it has been said "form *is* formless, formlessness *is* form."

The situation is somewhat similar to a mountain having a particular name to the natives on one side of it, but a different name to the residents on the other side of it.

Every form — whether a material body or an immaterial thought — has a beginning and an end: every form is impermanent. That which each form begins in, and ends in, is infinitely present: it is permanent. Whatever we say is real, or true, must *always* be real, permanently true.

Therefore, by comparison, the absolute is real, the transitory relative is said to be unreal. As a consequence, it is said that all forms are relative appearances on the background of the absolute actuality. In other words, if I build a house, it stands on what was empty space.

Among these *appearances* of reality are the human body, its mind, thoughts, and actions. These appearances serve functions during what one considers to be one's "lifetime". It is through the process of *mentation* by which we conceive the *divisions* which allow us to designate the multiple *forms* (which we manipulate on a daily basis in order to provide sustenance for the body). The primal *thought* would likely be "I need..."— whether the body needs food, shelter, clothing, or whatever.

Our practical thoughts begin with "I"; and where there is me, there is considered to be my body, my mind, my thoughts, my activities. In other words, viewing separative forms — multiplicity, duality — is a function of the discriminating mind. Once there is me, there are then those who are not me, "others." While such distinctions have practical value, they also lead to conflict: us versus them.

There is a period for each of us in which our divisive mind is absent: each night, scientists tell us, we experience deep, dreamless sleep. In the deep sleep condition, there are no thoughts of self, others, world, universe or anything else: no forms are present, there are no names — neither the "relative" nor the "absolute" is known to exist. We are in a state of total and complete emptiness. If you were to die while in this condition, there would be no "you" present to acknowledge the absence.

This condition of empty presence was that of the embryo before the formation of mentation. Upon the death of the body, and its mentation, this empty presence will continue to pertain. It's as if there was a terrifying tsunami, but yet there is never a mark which remains finally on the surface of the ocean.

This tells us that all which appears to exist during our "lifetime" is an illusion, as unreal as a sleeping dream and as "untrue".

So, the point of this discussion is to make clear that in an "empty" dream, it makes no matter what you (or "others") say, think, feel or do. Not anything ultimately matters.

Because existence is not established, there is no nonexistence; and since the two extremes do no exist, there is nothing in between.

Instructions to King Udayana

The Lowdown

Not anything has ever actually been created.

Not anything actually exists.

If we want to prove that something exists, we are confronted with the problem of dependent-arising: not anything can stand on its *own* as existent. All things depend on some other things for their (so-called) arising.

The phenomenon of dependent-arising itself depends upon someone to observe the phenomenon and declare that it exists. The person who makes that declaration has depended upon dependent-arising for *his* own arising and existence.

Something is not freely capable of existing on its own, when it depends upon some *other* thing for its existence. And the other thing upon which it depends is likewise not free-standing, because *it* is dependent upon something else for *its* existence.

Since all things are interdependently existent, not any thing is *real* in terms of being able to stand alone as self-existent. This tells us that not any thing can ever have been originated, from the very beginning.

Even dependent-arising does not exist as a reality. Obviously, if not anything has even been created, there are not things available to be dependent upon each other.

But for the person whose assumption it is that anything exists, the appearance that we designate dependent-arising can demonstrate that not any thing does actually exists *independently*, on its own.

And when not anything can be shown to be independently existent, one must conclude that not anything has ever actually been *created*.

What does seem to "exist" are appearances. These "real" appearances appear to a person who is himself dependently-arisen, and therefore not real. Can any thing an unreal person perceives be actually real?

Apart from the Dream itself, in which the dreamer himself is appearing, not anything is ever actually happening. Space does not exist, time does not exist, cause and effect do not exist, nor are there any phenomenon. Not any of these things exists, apart from the Dream itself—which does not *actually* exist, in reality.

Conventional Truth

Though forms—whether material or immaterial—are empty of reality and do not exist in the way they appear, unenlightened beings take them to be real. For even an enlightened being, who recognizes that forms are empty, avails himself in the day-to-day world of the *functionality* of forms, though he knows they are ultimately nonexistent. Thus, in this way, such things can be said to 'exist' as *conventional* 'truth'.

Emptiness, the underlying condition of all forms and phenomena, is the *ultimate* truth. The unenlightened person is limited to the conventional truth—which is not actually the real truth, but an illusion in the same way that a person can *truthfully* claim to have seen a mirage. The enlightened person accesses simultaneously the ultimate truth along with the conventional 'truth'.

However, for those who are familiar with the teaching of "no production" or "no creation" or "no origination," forms and phenomena are empty of reality, or existence, having not ever actually been created or produced at all, at any time.

From this standpoint, the distinctions between conventional and ultimate truth are moot. In total emptiness, no "truths" exist; not any of the named things exist. Emptiness is absolute.

And of complete emptiness, all that can be said is that it is empty; even to say that it 'exists' (or doesn't exist) is to say too much.

Gita Basics

Take ideas which are commonly accepted and which seem to be incontrovertible and question them. Turn them inside out and see what would happen if they were thought about in another way.

–Alan Watts

The Dalai Lama has said:

> In the 1960s, during the first decade of my life as an exile in India, I was able to delve deeply, and very personally, into the philosophy of emptiness.

What he learned came as a shock:

> Suddenly, it was as if lightning moved through my chest. I was so awestruck that, over the next few weeks, whenever I saw people, they seemed like a magician's illusion in that they appeared to inherently exist but I knew that they actually did not.

Emptiness (also known as sunyata, or ajata) was mainly propounded by the 2nd century Indian monk Nagarjuna, extrapolating logically from Buddha's core six-word teaching, "form is emptiness, emptiness is form." Madhyamaka, as these teachings were called, was the subject of the Dalai Lama's study: every thing in the universe is *empty* of true, independent reality (or, "inherent self-existence")—meaning they do not actually exist.

Geshe Kelsang Gyatso says:

> Therefore, if a practitioner is sincerely interested in traveling the path to enlightenment, he or she must make a concerted effort to understand the view of Nagarjuna and train in the wisdom realizing the *emptiness* of true, inherent self-existence.

From mankind's earliest writings, there have been those who sought to know the nature of that which has been described (though by many names) as the Absolute, or ultimate reality.

In the *Prajnaparamita* it says, "Only the awakened mind can comprehend it." But as Longchenpa has said, "to claim that it is unfathomable is a fool's attitude."

Nagarjuna wrote:

> Realising that this doctrine is too
>
> Profound and hard to understand,
>
> The Buddha, the Subduer,
>
> Turned away from teaching it.

Buddha began speaking of sunyata in his later years. Barry Kerzin writes:

> For the sake of beings of lesser intelligence, the Buddha taught that things "exist" truly. For the sake of beings of higher intelligence, he taught that nothing exists truly.

Buddhism was eventually driven out of India, and significant treatises found their way to Tibet. Only within about the last seventy-five years have translations appeared in the West, under the generic title "Madhyamaka" (or Madhyamika).

Author Edward Conze remarks ("wisdom" = emptiness):

> In fact, those who want to lean about wisdom must of necessity draw on the tradition of the fairly remote past. For *centuries* almost everyone has been silent on the subject.

Buddha, in fact, had once commented that his teachings on sunyata would likely die out, due to the difficulty of understanding them.

Mervyn Sprung notes:

> Madhyamika thought has been virulently controversial from the beginning, arousing misunderstanding, disbelief and outrage in roughly equal measure.

Andy Karr advises:

> Since it is one of the most profound and unfamiliar topics, we need many explanations and much study to come to terms with it.

And Jay Garfield assures:

> Madhyamika system depends directly on how one understands the concept of emptiness. If that is understood correctly, *everything* else falls into place.

If "ultimate reality" (or Reality) actually exists, how is it different from everything else?

Crosby and Skilton assert:

> For something 'to exist really' it must be *permanent, unchanging* and *independent* of other factors.

"Unchanging" is its most obvious description. What we characterize as *real* or *true* cannot be subject to fluctuation, dependably real every day of the week except for Mondays and Wednesdays. Real means *real*, unwaveringly; never *not* real, whether unpredictably or predictably. Reality, like it or not, is *always* Reality. In other words it is *permanently unchanging*.

Khenpo Tsultrim Gyamtso adds that:

> It would have to exist without *depending* on anything else, and be impervious to *causes* and conditions acting upon it.

This unique characteristic, independence, is the key to what makes reality *changeless*: it is impervious to any thing acting upon it which *could* change it; and that includes any other presumed "reality," such as, for example, time.

While conditions change, the reality *within* which conditions change is itself changeless. Reality, in other words, is independent of the *effects* of such elements as time, space or causation. Because reality is independently permanent, it does not go away. That is not true of any element in the universe; all of these are impermanent, subject to change (including the universe itself). Reality, however, is eternal.

Ken Wilber points out:

> That which is not ever-present cannot be ultimately real; the ultimately real is not something that can have a beginning in time, since that would make it strictly temporal, not timeless or eternal.

Ultimate reality, therefore, is ever-present, or permanent, and completely unaffected by any sources or phenomenon; independent in a way that not any thing else is. Being changeless, its *existence* is not dependent on any thing else either.

How does that compare with the myriad things which occur within reality, the relative or "conventional" objects and events, the forms and phenomena? These are not changeless, therefore they are not eternally present. Nor are they independent of the *effects* of any causes or conditions.

In fact, this last sentence tells us that all things, whether animate or inanimate, are "dependently originated"; that is, not any relative thing would exist but for the existence of some other things.

In other words, they do not *exist* in the way that what is *real* exists. When you begin to look at this closely, it means that all universal things are actually outside of the pole of being real in an independent or objective way; and what is not real, does not actually and objectively *exist* either.

That is, the universe and what appears in it is of the nature of illusion. All things are "empty of reality", as is an illusion.

Liu and Berger explain:

> For a proponent of Madhyamaka, *things* arise, change, and cease, completely dependent on various causes and conditions. They are dependently-originated, and thus never self-existent. Further, things are thoroughly impermanent and ever-changing, Thus, things

are empty of any independent and unchanging existence or nature. They are then not substantially *existent*. Consequently, Indian Madhyamaka holds that things are empty and *illusory*.

An illusion appears to have reality, but *appearance* and *reality* are not equivalently the same.

Of things which are mutually-dependent, says Shantideva, "as they exist by the power of each other, neither would be truly existent".

Gen Lamrimpa agrees that:

> As soon as we posit something as being affected, modified, or influenced by other phenomena, there is no way to assert that it is independent; and that means it cannot be truly existent or autonomous.

Tsultrim Gyamtso points out:

> That they *appear* does not cause them to be truly existent; and that they do not truly *exist* does not prevent them from appearing, just as is the case with appearances in dreams.

He adds,

> People who want to say that things truly exist will point to lots of things that seem real, like rocks, diamonds, and mountains. For the proponents of the Middle Way, however, rocks, diamonds, and mountains just prove their own point, because they are just as empty as everything else.... things in *conventional* reality exist as dependent-ly-arisen, mere *appearances*. Therefore, to say that conventional appearances 'exist' does not imply that they are *real*—they are simply mere appearances that occur due to the coming

together of causes and conditions, like dreams, illusions.

Thrangu Rinpoche has said:

> All appearances and all resultant conditions are illusory with no nature of their own, based on *previous* conditions that were equally illusory. This continuum of occurring appearances is unerring in so far as nothing ever occurs from outside of it; everything always occurs *within* this illusory structure of successive causes and conditions.

As Buddha summarizes:

> All 'things' are unreal; they are deceptions.

That is the point of Madhyamaka, sunyata, ajata: "all things are unreal". The Dalai Lama and I are the same age, 85. The Dalai Lama learned this point around 55 years ago, I learned this point about 20 years later. The general, common teaching of spiritual truth has yet to catch up.

Ken Wilber has noted:

> Waking Up schools have become out of touch, out of date, outmoded in certain ways, by simply failing to continue to add new and profoundly important truths to their own teachings.

Geshe Kelsang Gyatso:

> The experience of realizing emptiness can therefore be compared to waking up. Once we realize emptiness, we see clearly and without any doubt that the world, as we experienced it before, was deceptive and false.

Here is the important point, from Shantideva:

> Although it is unreal, a mirage can be seen;
>
> And that which *sees* is just the same.

We live in an unreal universe of our (individual and collective) imagination. What each of us sees is not real. But the seer itself cannot be real either. Because the *seer* is unreal, the things *seen*, or experienced, cannot therefore be real.

All serious spiritual teachings have always told us, as the Dalai Lama says:

> This "I" does not exist. When this fact is seen, the root misconception is counteracted, whereas if you *leave* that "I" as if it exists and *continue* with your analysis, you will not get down to the level of the root problem.

If you do not exist, your having been "born" is part of the illusive nature of your "life"; and likewise your unreal "death".

Nagarjuna:

> When thoughts of "I" and "mine" extinguish...
>
> As it ceases, so does birth...
>
> From 'existence' arises birth. From birth,
>
> certainly will arise aging, death...
>
> Since one cannot happen before the others,
>
> And they cannot happen simultaneously,
>
> Why would you ever think
>
> That birth, aging, and death truly exist?

Shantideva says that both death *and* living are equal parts of the fiction:

> When therefore in one's dream one's son has died, the state of mind that thinks he is no more supplants the thought that he is living still. And yet *both* thoughts are equally deceptive.

If 'I', my life, and death are empty of reality, what of my "mind" and its "thoughts"?

Kelsang points out:

> If you want to say that external objects do not truly exist, you will also have to say that mind does not truly exist either... Even though external objects do not exist, nevertheless we generate inherently existent 'minds' to which they appear.

If the objects or phenomena are not real, how real are our thoughts about them? Jnanashwar:

> Merely thinking about something (either about something in the past or about something in the future) is futile because the object, about which there is thinking, simply does not exist.

Chandrakirti:

> Just as when dreaming, so here when awake, things are false... For us, mind does not exist even when dreaming... In short, the meaning you should understand is this – just as *objects* of mind do not exist, mind *also* does not exist.

Shantideva couldn't have known that physicists would prove that atoms are as empty of substance as are whirlpools.

> These parts themselves will break down into atoms, and atoms will divide according to direc-

tions. These fragments, too, will also fall to nothing. Thus atoms are like empty space; they have no real existence.

Nagarjuna:

Like a dream, like an illusion,

Like a city of gandharvas [gremlins],

That's how birth and that's how living,

That's how dying are taught to be.

Dalai Lama:

By seeing that the true nature of things is impermanence, you will not be shocked by change when it occurs, not even by death.

Buddha:

Sentient beings do not exist, so no *life* force can be found either.

Nirvana's Depth

When shall I reveal this truth of emptiness
To those who go to ruin through belief in real existence?
– Shantideva

Those who seek *nirvana* come to learn that the word means "to snuff out," as one would snuff out a candle: it means to bring the "self" to an end.

The consequence is that when the idea of "me" has ended, the idea of all that is "not me"—that is, the world or universe, and all "other than me" that is *in* it—also comes to an end.

When we've recognized that the appearance that we call "I" is false, we likewise recognize that every "you" is equally false. And it is this "I" or "you" which is the *perceptor* of its universe. An unreal "person" is perceiving the environment supporting it—which must also be false, or equally unreal.

So, it is not that the person and the world are the same one thing (the Absolute), as we originally conclude. Neither the perceiver nor the perceived have ever actually existed as a fact, apart from an *illusionary* appearance by an *impermanent* seer. Where neither the seer nor the seen has existed in reality, the two are indeed the same—but the "same" is not a thing, it is *nothing*. The "thing" that it is, as the Buddhist puts it, is *empty* of Reality. That is to say, there is no person or world, in reality, which can transmute into an Absolute. It is an Absolute which permeates a universe that does not, in truth, have existence.

So, the "snuff out" of nirvana is to begin with the self, follow logic, and snuff out as well the *universe* of the self.

No Relationships

Enquirers have been shown, by Nargarjuna (and others), that not anything can ever have been created or originated; that any thing—material or not—which appears to exist in (and including) the universe actually lacks reality. Thus, all that appears to exist is, in truth, an illusion. This conclusion is known as *ajata* ("no creation").

The tendency of a human being studying this conclusion is to take it for granted that while the perceived is what is referred to as an illusion, the perceiver himself is not *within* the illusion. As a consequence, there are those who have attempted to "explain" the illusion as having been created by the "mind". Such a viewpoint is not a conclusion of ajata.

Not anything has ever been created: all is an illusion. What has not been created is not substantially real. Real means "what is existent"; so, what is not real does not actually exist. What appears to be real may be said to exist, but an *appearance* of reality is no more real than the appearance of an illusion.

You are in the illusory universe (or Dream); you are not outside of the illusion. Whatever the appearance, you— as with all things—are not substantially real; therefore, neither is your mind. Your unreal mind is not *creating* an unreal universe: neither of these has ever existed.

A sleeping dream is not *real*; it is not *caused* by an unreal mind. Both are simply expressive of the totality of the illusion, or Dream.

Causation itself is an *element* of the Dream. There can be no cause of something (and some thing else which is effected) where there is not one thing which has maintained reality. Causation, like any thing else within the Dream, is empty of reality, or actuality.

As a consequence, this applies as well to "relationships". A relationship cannot be real where there are no two, or more, entities which truly exist to *be* relatable.

Again, there is no actual relationship between the mind and the universe. No universe has been created, nor mind *within* it.

Unwinding Paradox

Our eyes and mind tell us that a mirage is, for example, a place where we may quench our thirst. Because, in fact, we cannot actually do so, we name it a mirage.

So, is there such a thing that appears to us as a mirage? Yes. Is it actual, or real, in that it contains drinkable water? No.

An *appearance* may seem to be real but aside from its appearance as such, it can have no reality.

It is our eyes which see an appearance, it is our mind which declares that what we see is actually real.

No phenomenon is entirely independent. If nothing else, it depends on some other thing for its birth or creation. It has been said that we are the cause of everything that we see or experience. If I look out and see a tree, for instance, it is my mind which tells me that I am looking at a tree. We, in our minds, give birth to every thing that we claim exists and is real. (This includes ourself.)

All things, including ourself, are "dependently arisen". In other words, not anything independently arises of its own volition, not any thing is entirely self-controlled or self-governed, or even totally self-defined. However, appearances may seem otherwise.

If there were something that could arise by its very own volition, then—by its own volition—it could determine to ever remain the same, to not change. Yet, there is not any *thing* that we know of which is not finally impermanent.

As Nagarjuna says:

> Never is there anywhere the existence of any-
> thing that is not dependently originated, hence
> never is there anything anywhere that is eternal.

If there were something which was ultimately real, it would not depend upon our minds for its existence: it would not be dependently arisen. Nor would the ultimate actuality change or cease to be.

Things which have an origination, and which change or age, are impermanent and finally cease to be: what has a beginning, has an ending. What does not cease to be (does not go out of existence) has not *come into existence*. It is permanent because it is unchanging. Unchanging, it knows neither the state of birth *nor* death.

All *things*, except for ultimate reality, are impermanent. Ultimate reality is not one of those things: it is no thing. Nothing. It is empty of any appearance; it is empty of any thing of any kind. It is empty of any description, including "existent" (or "nonexistent"). It is empty of origination, or cessation. At best, ultimate reality is total, complete emptiness.

Nagarjuna:

> Arising and dissolution do not hold with respect
> to that which is empty....
>
> Arising does not at all exist either with or without
> dissolution....

It is not right to say that there is the act of *origination*, whether of the existent, of the nonexistent, or of what both exists and does not exist....

Co-authors Mark Siderits and Shoryu Katsura write,

According to Madhyamaka, ultimate reality does not contain anything that arises. (And since Buddists generally agree that there are no eternal entities, this would mean that ultimate reality contains no entities whatsoever.) The realization of emptiness would then be insight into the true character of reality: that it is utterly devoid of existing entities.

But, despite the emptiness of ultimate reality, there are what do seem to be appearances. Would the true actuality of these appearances be emptiness?

The emptiness of ultimate reality cannot be just an appearance. Put another way, an appearance cannot be ultimate reality.

An appearance is just that: non real. All phenomena are empty of reality. Yet they do seemingly continue to appear.

So, emptiness is not apart from phenomena, and phenomena are not apart from emptiness. The appearance of phenomena can be said to have an origination; emptiness does not. Phenomena can be said to exist or not exist; emptiness *transcends* such descriptions.

The point of this is to recognize that all things which we say *are*, ultimately are absent of true reality whatsoever. All that is, is empty. Only one thing could be supposed to be real, and that is emptiness.

All appearances are empty and unreal: you; your mind; anything which this mind identifies, whether substantial or insubstantial; others; the world; the universe; this present moment; life; death; eternity.

The final recognition is that emptiness itself is empty of any qualities or attributes, even "reality" or "unreality", "true" or "not true".

There is, in truth, no right or wrong, good or bad. Ultimately, not anything matters; there is no entity to whom anything *could* matter.

Going Deeper

The rediscovery of ajata, in about the past 70 years, has produced much writing about it, but most writers simply repeat the fundamental points which were posited by Nagarjuna. Future awakened writers will likely produce original extrapolations from those fundamental points. Initially, these writers will likely need to explain the relationship between emptiness and worldly objects, until their readers understand that *ajata* means "no creation": or, emptiness actually invalidates the creation of any worldly phenomenon one could be concerned about.

In that endeavor, here's what ajata tells us about the presumed world, and universe.

It is not that there is "something" *truly* existing which is empty of reality; it is that there exists, in reality, "no thing" and that *is* what emptiness is.

Ajata is to walk into a canyon holding onto your ideas of "life" and "death"; make a complete turnaround, and walk back out, now fearless.

Our conditioning is based on (unquestioned) assumptions and faulty premises. We speak, for example, of atomic particles which reportedly are "smashed" together in laboratories. There are no atomic "particles" that possess an encasing structure of substance: they are actually more like force fields; think of a whirlpool.

At twilight, a piece of rope might be mistaken for a snake. You look again and recognize that it is actually a piece of rope. Yet *neither* object is real in the ultimate sense. Both are merely unreal worldly objects, *appearing* to have reality.

We look at our face in the mirror and suppose that it and its reflection are both "realities", even though one may be "more" so than the other. But from the standpoint of ultimate reality, of course, neither are real.

There is only an action where there is an actor; there is only an actor where there has been an action; neither can claim for itself the *independence* of a reality that is not dependent upon anything else in order to exist.

Reasoning itself is a phenomenon *within* the "worldly" dream, as are all that could be reasoned about, and the reasoner too. In other words, logic as well is not real, but then none of the things it supposedly applies to are real either. The fact of emptiness shows that logic too is empty, so *it* cannot answer any "why" or "how" questions one might expect to pose.

Imagination also is empty, yet it is *imagining* reality that occupies us throughout the Dream.

Unexpectedly, the answer to the "why" question is not affirmative, but negative: neti, neti; "not this, not that".

There is an approach that can lead us to the fact of the emptiness of the world: investigating its reality is its negation. The emptiness of the world presents that opportunity. Emptiness has no intention for us to discover it; it is the world of forms that points the way to the "why?"

Why is the world an "illusion"?; because it is empty of reality. Emptiness renders the world illusory; the illusion and its "why" question lead us into the ultimate truth.

Appearance of form causes us to assume that we are perceiving "reality". But paradoxically, *reality* is actually the *lack* of "reality".

What we think of as real things, we think of as arising *with* their reality. But ultimate Reality does not "arise". Anything which arises also departs; meanwhile it is changeable. Ultimate reality, being changeless, does not "depart"; neither does it arise, being "without beginning or end".

Though true reality is permanent, it does not disallow impermanent *appearances,* phenomena or forms. However, illusory forms cannot lay claim to ultimate reality, "arising" and "departing" as we suppose they do.

That all things are empty means that they are all the same. Even from this standpoint, "co-dependence" can be seen to be problematic because there are not really "co's".

An apple is the cause of an apple seed. The effect, the apple seed, causes an apple. These are the so-called "causes and conditions" of dependent origination.

The point of ajata is that all things are empty of reality, since every "form is emptiness" from its formation. Dependent arising, therefore, is a roundabout analogy for the means of *explaining* emptiness to those unwilling to accept that no forms have ever *actually* been formed, from the start.

All "things"—form, phenomena—can be seen to be co-dependent, and as such are impermanent; "things" change. Ultimate reality cannot be something which changes. It is the changelessness of ultimate reality that makes it really *Real*. "Things", then, are *empty* of reality.

Ajata shows us that both *non*existence and *seeming* existence are elements of all of the universal objects. Emptiness and phenomena (objects, actions, events) are two names for the same presentation.

Without forms (*we* are forms), emptiness would not be revealed. Without emptiness, forms would not have the *appearance* of existing.

Forms and Emptiness are not "two things" apart, existing free of each other.

Nagarjuna:

> Except for there being the cause of form,
> Form would not be seen.
> Except for there being what we call "form,"
> The cause of form would not appear either.

While forms, being empty, do not actually exist, our mind and conditioning insist that they do. However, since we are forms, *we* are not real (as with all forms in the universe, never having *actually* been originated, or created). Where I do not actually exist, beyond *appearing* to, neither does "my mind".

Knowing that there is no "me" (through advaita, or nonduality) is especially important because this is the gateway which can allow us to recognize the emptiness of every other form, and the "world". Emptiness, we could say, is something which can be acknowledged by the one who himself can acknowledge his own emptiness. While there might be the *thought* of an 'I', one recognizes that thoughts themselves are as unsubstantial as a dream or illusion. Our "being" as forms is indebted to emptiness.

Ultimate reality is another name for Final Truth: this means what can ultimately be ascertained from examining *worldly* "truth", or its lack of reality.

This investigation of worldly truth will result in what some will conclude to be a negative conclusion: form is *emptiness*. This doesn't mean that the world does not exist: it "exists" as *empty* of reality, as an illusion or dream.

A dream has "reality" in that it *appears*; it is *un*real in that its appearances do not mean anything ultimately, or really. In other words, the world exists in the same manner that a mirage exists: what "exists" *in* the world— such as "you"—exists in the same way you do *in* your sleeping dreams.

An unreal world is the consequence of a dream that is originated by a dreamer who is likewise unreal.

Looking at it from the standpoint of the Dream, it's fortunate that none of this "occurring" in the world is (and has, or will be) really *existing*.

So, everything we precede with "the" or "a" or "one", etc., is *within* the dualistic dream. All is empty of reality; and if we mistakenly identify emptiness as simply another "thing"—instead of what "things" are, which is emptiness—we're missing the point that emptiness too is *empty*; it too exists only as form, not ever "something" standing apart from it.

The world vanishes, with our realization of the nature of emptiness. But any idea that emptiness remains, or exists, must vanish too: emptiness *is* form.

This is why the shortest route to the answer to "why" is to recognize, from the beginning, that not any thing has ever been created or formed; period. Nothing to ask questions *about*.

Where there is no creation, there can only be nothing. Where there is nothing, there is no movement or activity. In other words, not anything has ever actually happened. This is the final realization.

> "Nobody goes anywhere."
> – artist Karin Frey

Getting "There" from Here

What is "relative" is "any thing or event (phenomenon) which depends upon something else for its identity or qualities; not absolute".

Any object or concept that is relative is a form; "a distinctive appearance indicating a particular separate entity as being finite".

And finite forms are "within a limitation; not infinite".

The limitation is that each form, or phenomenon, has a beginning somewhere in time or space, and thus an ending as well. In other words, forms have the characteristic of impermanence, in addition to dependence upon alternative things which define their separate identity as an entity.

This brings us to you: you, body and mind, are a relative form, an impermanent form, dependent on other entities or phenomenon.

Where there is a "you" and any "other thing" upon which your dependence relies, there are "two, or more, things": the condition of "duality", in spiritual terms. What is meant when the term "nonduality" is used, in this context?

An intuitive understanding of nonduality is said to be the experience of an enlightened, or Self-realized, person.

What a seeker of enlightenment can come to know is the basic, or ultimate, truth—the true reality of the nature of existence in this universe: and thus all that is within it, including oneself. It is the answer to the spiritual question "Who am I?"

Obviously, anything which is definable as "relative" (any two or more things) is not nondual. Therefore, the *nondual* is not a form, entity, object, thing or event (it is a noumenon). Being (or occuring) beyond form, it would be form-less.

Being formless, it would not be finite, nor impermanent. It would be limitless, without beginning or end in time or space.

Without boundaries, barriers, restrictions, or restraints, it would be *omnipresent*, beyond relationship to time or space. Being formless, it would not know separation, in time or space.

Unlike the appearance of forms, it would have no appearance or identity, in particular, by qualities. Being formless it would be independent of any other thing that would define it.

And because it was not dependent on any other thing, it would not be affected by changes.

Being formless and thus unrestrained by time or space (as are forms) and being limitless, all that is limited would need to appear within its infinity. All changes must lie within the field which is change-less. Whatever is impermanent must be bounded by the single thing which is permanent, or Eternal.

An ultimate, fundamental Reality cannot be impermanent, a subject of change. The universe, and every thing
in it, is impermanent. Thus to know what is true, we do
not seek for Reality in the universe, but instead in the
omni-present Formlessness.

The Formless is Reality; every relative thing is not. But
what if the "two" aren't *different* in their "essential
nature"?

The unrestricted formlessness, being omnipresent, must
surround every form. But being unrestrained by any
border or barriers, it must also penetrate, permeate and
saturate every form. In other words, "no where is it not",
externally or internally.

So all that is relative (the entire universe) must be within
the omnipresent formlessness, at the very same time that
formlessness is *within* everything relative.

To speak of that which is formless is the same thing as to
speak of emptiness. It is not a thing (or event); is without
any qualities; is beyond even the forms of space and
time, and cause-and-effect; is changeless and thus *ever*
present; and being an unchanging condition is the only
actual, ultimate Reality.

With not anything that is outside of, or apart from, the
primordially ultimate condition of emptiness, every form
in its *formation* is formed in emptiness. It is this condition which immediately lends each form its "reality" as
long as it continues to exist.

This is why it is maintained in Buddha's *Heart Sutra* that
"form is emptiness, emptiness is form."

Your reality is that you are a form. Every form in the universe begins, endures, and ends within the ultimate Reality of the presence of Emptiness.

Emptiness is the Reality; relative forms are dependent upon it for their impermanent existence.

Emptiness is...

Understanding sunyata is not difficult, once it has been clearly explained. The difficulty is for the one who is attempting to clearly explain it. A clear explanation is usually a rational explanation. But the subject of emptiness does not fit into the category of either reasonable or not reasonable, it being empty of qualities. The Dream—of birth, life, and death—is made up of objects and events, each an impermanent form. Being impermanent and co-dependent, no form in the Dream possesses the attribute of ever-presence that would be required in order to qualify as ultimately real. Forms appear to be real, to the perceiver; but the perceiver—being a form—is likewise unreal. The entire Dream itself is unreal, produced by an unreal dreamer; an illusion; not any thing actually exists, in reality.

Instruction in ajata tells us initially, "emptiness is form" (Heart Sutra). Eventually, we come to recognize that forms do not actually exist. We have, in truth, been told this by the name *ajata*, which means (from Sanskrit) "no creation"; not any thing, or form, has ever been created or originated from the very start.

Because forms are *unreal*, they have never originated from anything anywhere. That is why the supposed appearance of objects and events is called a Dream;

phenomena in the perceived universe have no more reality than the fixture of a dream.

Where not anything has existed from the start, the start is totally empty. Not anything "comes out of" emptiness.

To say that emptiness is form and forms do not exist is as good as saying "nor does emptiness exist". That is the final point of ajata: of *emptiness*, there is not anything about which one could assert either an "existence" or a "nonexistence". Any such descriptive terms must be moot.

This is why the final reality can be summed up by Geshe Tashi Tsering in three simple words:

Nothing exists ultimately.

Who is Asking Why?

From the Upanishads on down, there have been sages who have discovered the meaning of ajata's message, and have declared "no creation" or "no origination" or "no birth" etc.

They are stating that the nature of ultimate reality is emptiness or nothingness or a void, and that from a "condition" of emptiness not anything can ever come out or originate or be born.

In other words, any thing which appears to exist is not, and cannot be, a creation from nothingness. Put another way, any thing which seems to appear is not real, from the ultimate standpoint.

This is not a denial that things do seem to appear. Both anything which seems to appear and the person to whom they seem to appear are unreal.

The analogy which is classically given is that of a sleeping dream. In the dream, you—a figure which is not actually real—interact in a world which does not actually exist.

In this analogy, when you—whom ajata says cannot have had this existence from the start—wake up from the sleeping dream, you are nevertheless an unreal person seeming to live in a world which does not exist in actuality. In other words, the waking "dream" is a continuation of the sleeping dream. Neither one can be any more real than the other.

Another way in which the literature puts this is to say that all forms are empty. Anything which is truly empty cannot be said to "exist"; and where existence is out of the question, "not exists" is not applicable. You, as a form, are empty. The world, as a form, is empty. In other words, both are nothing. Both have not ever been created, or originated. Though they seem to appear (within the big Dream), both are without any actual reality.

The seeming person continues to live out her life (from supposed "birth" to "death") in a seeming world, in a seeming universe.

Yet, in what could be said to be the true or ultimate reality of emptiness, not anything ever has, or could, happen. From the ultimate standpoint, there is not anything that ever needs to be explained.

Any questions which arise and any answers are within the Dream—and the Dream is not real.

Those who understand this, the sages would say, have awakened from the big Dream. Whether one does or does not, in the end, makes absolutely no difference.

But for those who do awaken, all their questions—within the Dream—are seen to be utterly empty, and meaningless.

Six Simple Words

The six-word formula—"form is emptiness, emptiness is form"—causes more confusion than it needs to. Let's walk through it.

Where form—that is, all phenomena—is *emptiness*, form does not itself exist. Form, yes, *appears* to exist, because "we" see it, and name it as such.

But "we" are forms; *we* do not exist. What does not exist is claiming to see what is equally non-existent. What *does* exist? Not any thing: all is empty.

So, forms—phenomena—are said to exist, and likewise are also said to be empty of existence. Emptiness is not something which has been *added* to existing forms: emptiness is what forms *are*, from start to finish.

Emptiness being the ultimate condition, not any thing has ever actually been created from what is an empty condition: not any things exists, in actuality. Thus, what appear to be forms are emptiness.

If there were no (supposedly real) forms, emptiness would not exist—because emptiness does not "exist."

"We" say that emptiness exists, and so in that sense it appears to exist (i.e., "Emptiness is what forms are.") But *emptiness* itself cannot be said either to be "non-existent" nor "existent": if there were no *minds* in the universe, where would such a distinction come from?

Emptiness does not even exist as forms: there are no *real* forms.

What appear as forms are impermanent. We cannot say of emptiness that it is either "permanent" or "impermanent". It does not "exist" (or "nonexist").

However, of forms we can say that they *appear* to exist, but in actuality do not exist.

All that you need to know is that all phenomena—material or non-material—are empty of existence, beyond their appearance. This includes you, and your world.

> Be mindful that everything, the moving and the unmoving, is naturally empty from the beginning.
>
> —Darikapa

As the Samadhiraja says: "To not see anything is to see all phenomena."

> There is nothing to be removed from it;
> There is nothing whatsoever to be added.
> Reality should be viewed correctly.
> When reality is seen, one is liberated.
> —Asango

Not a Thing

"Emptiness is form, form is emptiness." Form does not *originate* and then emptiness comes from somewhere and "fills" it.

The point of this is that when form *appears*, it is an "appearance" because it is *empty*, empty of *reality*; every form is false, because all forms are empty of reality.

Emptiness is the ultimate condition; it *is* what is, because there is not any thing that is not it.

But emptiness is not a standing field, such as the field of gravity. Not only is it absent a relationship with time or space, but its presence is to be "noticed" only in explaining why forms are appearances that, in truth, lack inherent reality.

A form is an apparent "thing"; emptiness is not a thing: it is what all things apparently are, but because things are not real, the seeming "cause" of their existence cannot be existent either.

This is *why* it is said that emptiness itself does not "exist"; and does not *not* exist, because ultimately there is no other condition.

This understanding is important, because seekers tend to think of emptiness as an "it", an entity not unlike a form; thus, sentence two at the top.

Even though it has been stated that total emptiness can not contain any "qualities", or quantities, seekers like to insist that it must at least have the nature of some "thingness" about it: for instance, it must at least represent "be-ing".

But for any thing to be, it must in truth exist. The "existence" of emptiness is only as its presence in *transient* forms; forms are false, the "existence" of emptiness is also false, as an entity.

Therefore, emptiness does not *exist* as an entity, an It, or as Being.

A to Z

Real, in spiritual texts, is sometimes spelled with a capital R. That which is real exists in *fact,* it's actual, not merely seeming or possible.

A synonym is "true": certain, accurate, constant.

That which is real and true is not subject to impermanence or equivocation, not uncertain or malleable.

"What is truly real?" has been the perennial question of mankind. What is the ultimate essence or nature of this universe? What is really, truly existent, without a doubt?

Traditionally, this has been a matter of belief or faith, but these remain in the category of seeming, or possible; uncertain. The signs are there, that can tell us rationally what truly exists.

When we are looking for the truth, we know that it must lay at the bottom of the questions. The questions may change with time, but ultimate reality—the "answer"—must be fundamental and unchanging. *Ultimate* means conclusive; that beyond which one cannot go.

The underlying truth of reality is not subject to change, as are all of the other things which depend upon that truth. Each of these other things may exist or not exist, but fundamental truth, reality, does not waver in its presence.

That which is unceasingly constant is eternal, outside of the erosion of time, beyond beginnings or endings.

Being immobile, truth is self-sustaining, independent of extraneous conditions or the effects of any causes that could amend it.

Those things which have a beginning (or are born) and have an ending (or die) are said to "exist", to occur, to have being or life or form. That which has no beginning or ending in time, or space, would be free of form. It would not be proper to say that it either exists or does not exist.

We know that our universe is a form within time, because it changes; change is a universal effect of time. So, the universe and everything in it is dependent upon the timeless, fundamental, formless ultimate reality, which does not change.

None of the things in the universe are independent of every other thing. Everything is affected by conditions and causes; creation and destruction, for example; change at the very least. Not any occurrence is entirely of itself, nor beyond impermanence.

Nor are any of the things in the universe outside of—or absent from—the changeless ultimate reality. There is not a foreground that can be apart from its background.

To summarize at this point, the universe and its contents are each a form which has a beginning and ending—with a life, or being, in between—existing in time, dependent upon *conditions* such as change and impermanence. In the sense of being truly real, these things are not truly real.

That which is real is formless, without beginning or ending, timeless, independent of conditions or causes; and stand-alone, changeless, neither existing or not existing: *beyond* which one cannot go.

This is reality, this is truth. What one-word name can we give it? Since it is empty of any positive or identifiable characteristics, it is known as emptiness.

Out of the state of emptiness—nothingness or void— what can emerge or arise or be created? Only nothing can be created from nothingness. It cannot be the source of anything; without content, conditions or causes within it. Emptiness is not the source of anything. It is the underlying fundamental or ultimate reality of truth.

Then from whence has arisen the cosmos and its content? Not *anything* has arisen: they do not have reality. The unreal has not been *created*.

You are in the universe: the universe, and what is in it, are not truly real; hence, you are not real. Being unreal, all that anyone perceives is equally unreal, from the cosmos on down, and including oneself.

That which *is* real, emptiness, has not created or sourced what is unreal. Emptiness is the fundamental, underlying and ultimate state upon which the cosmos and its unreal contents rest. All *things*—including you, and your life—are, it can be said, empty of reality. Unreal, *simultaneously* empty.

This, it can be understood, is real and true.

An analogy that is often made is that our experience while awake is no more real than our sleeping experience while dreaming, thus our entire worldly experience is a Dream, with a capital D. Everything is within that, from our presumed birth to our supposed death, every empty *plus* or *minus*, every imaginable me or you.

To live your life with this understanding is to "wake up" to (or within) the Dream.

Direct Conclusion

Looking at our universe from the viewpoint of physics, Dr. Robert Lanza says,

> Entanglement has proven time and space as meaningless.
>
> We've seen that, especially since the late 1990s, experiments have confirmed the reality of entanglement, where two bits of light or actual physical objects, even clumps of material that were created together, fly off and live separate lives, but are always "aware" of the other's status. If one is measured or observed, its twin knows this is happening and instantaneously assumes the guise of a particle or bit of light with complementary properties. This "information" traverses empty space with no time lag, even if the twins are on opposite sides of the galaxy. In short, space is penetrated instantaneously, in zero time, no matter the distance....
>
> It's amazing that this breakaway from classical physics is still relatively unknown by the public, even if most people do equate quantum theory with strangeness....
>
> We've already fully seen that neither space nor time are real in any sense except as appearances or tools of the mind. Thus, anything that seems to occupy space (like the brain or body) or endures in time (again, the brain and body) has no absolute reality, but only an apparent one, created by the mind....

$E = mc^2$ has been proven to precisely represent how mass is convertible into energy, while energy is convertible to mass. Effectively, the two elements of our universe cancel each other out. Thus, says astronomy professor Mark Whittle,

> The total mass/energy of the universe equals zero: the universe sums to nothing. This is comparable to what one associates with traditional spiritual-based cosmologies.

The universe sums to nothing: then what of the "creation" of the Big Bang, which *gave* us our universe? It couldn't have occurred in space or time; these presumed properties were allegedly *results* of the Big Bang.

"Where" could a Big Bang have occurred? Science writer Brad Lemley says to start "by imagining nothing, *don't* imagine outer space with nothing in it. Imagine no space at all." The Big Bang "wasn't the emergence of the universe *into* space, but rather the emergence of space," according to physicist Brian Clegg in *Before the Big Bang*. Prior to the Big Bang, there was "not empty space; just *nothing*."

Furthermore, physicists assert that space is, and has been, expanding. *Into* what can space be expanding? Into nothingness? Where would the boundary of "space" and "nothingness" meet, and how would they be distinguishable?

Physics is the *science* which investigates "reality" in our universe: it is a field of infinitely complex, unanswered (possibly unanswerable) questions.

To make their deliberations easier, physicists employ the principle of "Occam's razor": the simplest, least complicated and most direct solution to a dilemma is most likely its answer.

What could be more simple and direct than the conclusion—no more unprovable, but less improbable that the Big Bang creation story—that the universe, and everything in it, is an illusion in the mind of humans *within* the illusion, there having never been any thing other than an illusion *seeming* to have occurred, from the start?

That they appear does not cause them to be truly existent, and that they do not truly exist does not prevent them from appearing, just as is the case with appearances in dreams…

Emptiness is the deepest and most subtle topic one could ever attempt to understand, so it is never enough to hear or read teachings on emptiness just once.

Geshe Tashi Tsering

There's No Anywhere

The appearances of all phenomena, and related actions and events in the presumed universe, have equally in common their underlying emptiness. Therefore, there is only one key needed to unlock the mystery of ultimate reality: It *is* that all-embracing emptiness. All possible explanations are emptied of their importance, with the clear understanding of the overarching nature of emptiness.

All phenomenal appearances are dependent upon causes or conditions for their impermanent existence. Every form is formed as a result of its source, its cause. Emptiness, by definition, is formless; complete emptiness cannot be a *source* or cause of any thing, nor can emptiness be *caused* by any thing.

Any thing which is dependent upon a cause or condition, for its relative and impermanent existence, cannot in truth be the self-sustaining unchanging ever-present reality.

Only what is universally unchanging and not subject to conditions (such as impermanence) can ultimately be real. The cosmos and all of its forms of content are then unreal, in any really ultimate sense.

Therefore, the first basic lesson in the teaching of emptiness is that you (and every *other* you) are not real. As the literature puts it, you are "empty of reality". In light of the unique existence of ultimate reality, you "do not exist".

So, if all phenomena are actually false, no phenomena have *actually* been originated, or created. All things ultimately being empty, emptiness is form's real condition. The reason why you are not real, the teaching tells us, is because not any thing has ever actually manifested which is not dependent on other equally unreal conditional causes. You are empty of reality because not *anything* has ever actually arisen.

Because your appearance was not ever actually anything other than an unreal "creation", within an unreal universe, your dis-appearance would be equally the same. There is no *you* that has ever actually come and gone, anywhere. There is not, in fact, *even* an anywhere which has reality.

Isness to Emptiness

From the standpoint of understanding *advaita*, the problem people have is that realizing that "you" are the Absolute represents, in their psyche, one entity (you) merely being replaced by what they perceive is another (Absolute).

From the standpoint of *ajata*, where the Absolute may more clearly be recognized not to be an *entity*, because it is empty of any qualifying descriptions, this has not been a problem.

We each think we have an origin. We may be tempted to assume, then, that what we conclude "replaces" our being must similarly *originate* somewhere.

Ajata broadens our view to emphasize that emptiness cannot be viewed as an entity, nor can it be the subject of cause, or origination.

Emptiness is not an alternate or replacement for anything: all forms or phenomena *are* empty of the reality most people assume for them: it is their actual nature or essence. Because of that emptiness, it is why—as *with* emptiness—no supposed thing can have actually been originated.

Nagarjuna says it simply:

> Things do not arise at any place, at any time. ...
> origination, and so on, are illusory appearances.

Shantideva sums it up:

> There is but one truth, absence of all origin.

The forms which emptiness imbues appear outwardly to exist as real, but also appear—to the form of a human, which is equally empty—to have been originated as substantive entities. And emptiness is not some feature that has been added on to items, at a particular time or place; it is an underlying condition for forms' appearance, fundamentally.

Milarepa:

> What *defines* appearances is that they've never
> been born.

The Dalai Lama:

> Emptiness is not something made up by the mind;
> this is how things have been from the start.

The first important recognition, in ajata, is that *you* and emptiness are not apart. "Emptiness is form." "Form *is* emptiness."

If you presume that a form which *appears* or seems to be real must *actually* be real — in the sense of being eternally unchanging — then you are deluded.

As Tsultrim Rinpoche has stated:

> Like a dream appearance, the daytime forms,
> sounds, smells, tastes, and tactile sensations we
> perceive on the outside, as well as our thoughts
> and mental states within, are all mere appear-

ances that are empty of inherent nature, that do not truly exist...

When *you* do not truly exist, your mind, thoughts or consciousness—and therefore your activities—are not real either.

Nagarjuna:

> Sight and hearing and so forth, feeling and the rest—if what *possesses* them does not exist, *they* too do not exist.

The Dalai Lama:

> The sign that you have truly become impressed with the *absence* of the concrete, solid existence of the "I" occurs when you consider body or mind and no longer take their appearance to be true.

Karmapa Rangjung Dorje:

> As for the mind, there is no mind! Mind is empty of essence.

Tsultrim Rinpoche:

> The arising of thought is therefore empty of any inherent nature.

Buddha, speaking of the universe of appearances:

> With the cessation of consciousness, *this* is all destroyed.

We close our eyes for the last time and the world and universe disappear. To your knowledge, if you were to look back on an empty universe, you would not even know that you had ever existed, that birth and life and death were realities, or that anything had ever taken place at all.

Hui-Chung:

> But the mind and the world are empty. No matter how we think or act, nothing at all happens.

Tsultrim Rinpoche:

> However, in order to understand the true nature of reality, we must realize that nothing ever really happens. We must realize that arising and birth are not real.

So how do we live our life, when we are aware that the universe of appearances is as empty of actual reality as is a dream?

Kelsang Rinpoche:

> We can continue to perform our daily activities, yet at the same time remember that the things we normally 'see' do not exist... Nothing exists other than emptiness.

We *live* as if we are the actor in our sleeping dream each night, knowing that not anything — even "death" — need be taken seriously.

Donald S. Lopez Jr:

> The benefit of such reliance is that, by understanding the meaning of emptiness, one's mind is freed from all reasons of fear.

Krishnamurti:

> When there is the discovery, the experiencing, of that nothingness as you, then fear completely drops away.

Tulku Urgyen Rinpoche:

Because all appearances are ultimately empty and will vanish completely, we really don't have to worry about them.

Activity in the world is not truly enlightened unless it springs from the awareness that, in the absolute sense, nothing is being done or needs to be done...

If it were not for emptiness, nothing could appear at all. At the same time, if there were no appearances, there could be no emptiness.

Francesca Fremantle

Absolute as Reality

The purpose of *advaita* is to persuade us that—despite what we've been conditioned to believe—there are no separate individual entities: there is only one indivisible actuality, usually referred to in spiritual writings as the Absolute.

All seeming forms share this fundamental identity; every "you" in the cosmos is actually the Absolute, and all that's being done is the Absolute, doing what it does. There is no such thing as a "person", acting out of a ("his" or "her") unique will.

Those who've come to a realization that their separate identity is merely a mistaken fiction, overlain on an Absolute reality, can easily recognize that the condition which is true for them must also be true for all other supposed separate entities.

This is the basis of the "self" discovery, (there *is* no self) known as enlightenment.

It is important to arrive at this point, because knowing that "the self does not exist" is one of the consequences in learning about *ajata*.

However, in some advaita teachings, the Absolute is viewed not only as "who you really are", but as (also) the *source* of who you are, as well as the source of all other phenomena in the universe.

From the standpoint of ajata, meanwhile, the rationale for why you do not exist is, moreover, that not *any* thing has ever been created, or existent, from the very first: in other words, not any thing has ever *been* sourced. That is, the Absolute is not the source or creator of any thing which is said to have existed.

The only actual condition which has ever pertained, according to ajata, would be that of total and complete emptiness: all apparent forms are, in truth, "empty of reality", *empty* forms. The forms are not real, just as a particular form—the self—is not real. Forms are merely "seeming" forms; they can in no way have been produced, in reality, from a condition of emptiness.

So, while an advaitan might view a form and see it as the Absolute, the ajata viewer sees it as emptiness, "empty of reality". The form, to him, has not ever actually existed; therefore it has no reality, as the Absolute or anything else.

Therefore, the Absolute cannot be an ersatz stand-in, or proximate substitute, for the unreality of emptiness. In other words, emptiness is empty of all "realities", and this includes the conception of the Absolute.

Empty Universe

We are unreal dreamers living in an unreal world in an unreal universe; that is the Dream, with a capital D. While waking up to the nature of this Dream, while still *in* it, has no more ultimate reality than does the Dream itself, it can change the entire perspective of the dreamer to one of serenity on troubling questions—such as "How worrisome is death?"

Nagarjuna:

> To whom emptiness makes sense
> everything makes sense.
> To whom emptiness does not make sense
> nothing makes sense.

We can make no sense of "life as it is", because it actually isn't. Liu and Berger write:

> Once people understand that ultimate *reality* is *nothingness* or *emptiness*, they acquire levels of insight into their mundane existence that can *profoundly* change them. This insight, commonly spoken of as enlightenment, enables people to transcend their ordinary concerns in life.... Don't worry about the "existence" of emptiness, or how we can make any *true* statement about things that do no exist. What is said, or not said, is merely a way to get people to see the operation of *emptiness* in life. Emptiness is ineffable, because it simply is the state of *ineffability*.

I have spoken of (and used descriptive quotations of many writers on the subject) "ultimate reality". It must be changeless, and thus independent of any influencing condition or the effects of any outward causes.

Emptiness is not a replacement for 'what is', it is what is. Tashi Tsering:

> Emptiness is a nonaffirming negation; it negates true existence without presuming something else positive in its place.

The Dream itself constitutes empty appearances: "form is emptiness, emptiness is form". Illusory appearances *are* emptiness. Emptiness does not disallow illusive forms. The Dalai Lama:

> Emptiness is not something made up by the mind; this is how things have been from the start. Appearance and emptiness are *one* entity, and cannot be differentiated into separate entities.

Fletcher and Blankleder state:

> In fact, the ultimate is not separate from phenomena; it is the very nature of phenomena. The *ultimate* is what the *conventional* really is; the conventional is the way the ultimate appears.

Khenpo Tsultrim Gyamtso says,

> The phenomena of samsara and nirvana do not truly exist, and yet they still appear—there is a mere appearance of things, and that appearance is the union of appearance and emptiness.

Fletcher and Blankleder:

> The knowledge of the ultimate transcends thought. It is suprarational. It is nonconceptual and nondual—quite different, we may suppose,

from anything that we have ever experienced to date. It is *prajna*: immediate, *intuitive* insight into "such-ness," the wisdom of emptiness *beyond* subject and object.

At the end of the appearance of the Dream, in "death", whether we have awakened in it or not, there is a singular everlasting condition: emptiness. Emptiness is empty, there is not any thing "in" it. No 'I', for example. You will never know that you thought you had existed. You will never know that *any* thing had ever existed. From the ultimate standpoint, what difference does it make what you do, say, think or feel? None whatsoever. That is the liberation to be found in waking to the Dream.

Crosby and Skilton:

> What one must *realize* is the emptiness, sunyata, of all phenomena, including everything perceived as *constituting* the universe.

You may not want life to be meaningless, but remember: The fact that you want something to be true is not a reason to think it is. If the troubling *answers are the best answers we have, and they really do entail that life is meaningless—then life is meaningless.*

Professor David Johnson

No Mind, No Matter

Mankind's deepest search has been to know what is ultimately Real, the Truth. Reason tells us that final, absolute reality must always, everlastingly and changelessly, be undeniably real and true.

Of what do we know that is absolutely changeless and free of the effect of time? One thing only: a condition of emptiness, or nothingness, formlessness.

The search for reality or truth is a hopeful quest for meaning in our world and life. Scientifically, it has evolved into the field called physics. Physics purports to explain to us how, or why, the universe works. Given the difficulty of *proving* any proposition on a universal scale, these explanations are given on the basis of theories, which are subject to revision as evidence evolves.

The fundamental theory is called the Big Bang, currently. It says that our universe has grown over 13.8 billion years, from a point that was infinitely tiny. What developed, as with a "bang", was a spatial expansion, which was simultaneously the initiation of time (where there is space, time is necessary to traverse and measure it). Time and space are mutually dependent.

"Where" could this event have occurred? It couldn't have been in empty space: "space" was a product of the event. Could it have occurred in emptiness? Emptiness is totally empty; there is not any thing "in" a condition of absolute emptiness which can be an effector of any other condition or development.

Did the Big Bang event have a "cause"? If so, what was the cause of the *causer*?

Though not any thing can be generated out of a condition of total emptiness, where could a cause have found a location?

It is *change* that clarifies that not any thing in this universe can be real. Change means that not any thing is permanent or everlasting. Only one thing can be permanent, and that is ultimate reality. Only a condition of total and complete *emptiness* can be absolutely *changeless*.

Physics provides theories about the origin of the universe; the first *assumption* is that it has been caused. Cause and effect occur in time and space: cause and effect are a consequence which has to rely on the "real" presence of the universe itself.

All of science's explanations could be interesting (or even entertaining) if you suppose that the "universe" had *really* been "created". A more elegant recognition is that the true condition of emptiness remains the unperturbed Reality, and that the supposition of a changing and impermanent universe has no more reality than we ourselves—a product of this unreal universe.

We are unreal, the universe is unreal, life itself is unreal. There is no "meaning" in "life". The only lasting and true condition is emptiness.

"Right" Action

According to the theory of the origin of the universe, the universe began with an expansion, now known as the "Big Bang". Out of this expansion, space grew to become universal, and time evolved to measure the expansion from one point in space to another.

To be clear, the expansion was not *into* space, the expansion was the initiation of space. And time evolved *consequent* with the development of space.

All very well, but from *what* was the *causation* of the Big Bang? Any effect—such as expansion—is a result of one or another causes, according to scientific 'laws'. Yet causation, in our own universe, is one (of many) *effects* of the big bang *itself*.

In other words, an effect (e.g., expansion) is to be preceded by its cause. *Precede*, of course, means to "come before": cause and effect are in a relationship which depends, to some extent, on time. And time is dependent upon a development of *space*.

The point of this is that, *before* the effect of the big bang, there would be no element of *time* in which the *cause* of a big bang (or, expansion) could have an opportunity to occur.

Because every thing which is said to "exist" *in* the universe (*and* the "universe" as their enclosure) could not have been caused, or occurred, it is scientifically obvious that *existence* itself has not actually originated.

Because we assume that we are "real", we conclude that we are the actors (cause) of our myriad actions (effects).

But because cause-and-effect, and the time relationship these are dependent upon, could not have been involved in the (timeless pre-bang) "creation" of a *real* universe, cause-and-effect phenomena are no more real than any other supposed element in an uncreated universe.

In other words, not only are *we* not real, but neither are our actions nor any of their possible consequences.

If cause-and-effect had any ultimate reality, you (as causative actor) could choose to will that you live immortally, that you abolish your physical death eternally.

Yet, the truth is, you are not real nor are the presumed consequences of your—ultimately unreal—actions.

What, then, really *matters*? Not anything.

The Unreal Dream

Annette:

Another subtle point. If you say that we began in emptiness, "entering the Dream at our 'birth' and returning after our 'death,'" is this a *departure* of a self from the state or condition of emptiness, later to *return* to it?

Can something which is *unreal*, as you are, *truly* come from somewhere and later return to it?

"Form *is* emptiness." All *things* are empty of reality; in other words, do not truly exist. They are never *apart* from emptiness. If we were to ask, what is the *true* nature of any thing, it would be emptiness.

Forms do not "begin" *in* emptiness. Actual emptiness cannot create any thing. Emptiness is, we might say, the ground state. It is all that *is*; all else, such as forms, are a false appearance. Being *unreal*, they are not *created*. We, who are self-declared to be forms, are no more real than our birth and death, which are likewise empty of reality. As unreal forms, we can only contemplate an unreal world. *We* are the "creators" of the illusionary world, both it and us comprising and facilitating the Dream.

Emptiness does not "remain", at any point. It is, in *reality*, all that has ever actually "been"; nothing that any thing could *return* to.

The awareness of "emptiness" is not a blank loss of consciousness, an inanimate empty space; rather it is the cognition of daily life without attachment to it…

Thus the expression of "emptiness" is not the manifestation of Absolute Reality, the revelation of the Divine, but the means for dissipating the desire for such an Absolute.

Frederick Streng

Transparent Reality

To answer your simple question with a simple answer ("What *is* real?"): whatever we would consider to be real cannot be something which comes and goes; *that* excludes anything which is a form, either substantial (e.g., the universe) or insubstantial (a thought). All forms have a beginning, somewhere in time or space, and an ending: they come and they go.

What can be *depended* upon to not come and go is that which has never been *created*; that which we cannot say has ever had a beginning. Therefore, it would not be any thing or form.

Time and space, in which anything comes and goes, would have no relationship to this which is form-less.

As contrasted to every other thing, this would be no thing—which the scriptures call nothing, or nothingness (*ness* meaning "the condition of").

As no thing, it is empty of *being*. Thus, this condition is also called emptiness.

However, once you understand this, we can no longer say that the ultimate reality is emptiness. *Emptiness* would have to be empty of any *conditions*, such as "real" or "not real".

So instead we would say: the ultimate condition is emptiness, which is neither real nor unreal.

Not being either real or unreal, it has had no beginning, and does not come and go.

Within the Dream

The figure of speech "to live within the Dream," Cleo, means to assume that our (meaningless) "life" appears to be occurring in a world, and universe, which (like our life) we presume to be real or actual; both our life and its context are truly without reality, like an illusion. So, to that extent, we are "within" this Dream.

But the point of fact is that we are not really *within* anything, because what there appears to *be* is, in actuality, empty of reality; in other words, substantially non-existent.

This emptiness of all things is not a stand-apart, or separable, condition: it *is* what things, and their consequent events, *are*. "Form *is* emptiness."

So a similar figure of speech, "to go outside of the Dream," simply means to wake up to the fact (while living our "life") that neither "I" nor anything I sense or assume to be real, or exist, is actually anything other than total emptiness. Emptiness is, we might say, here now, as long as there is any form of any thing to be empty.

In the condition of emptiness, of course, there would neither really be an inside nor an outside. And neither would there actually be either of these two conditions, in truth, applied to the Dream, since the Dream *itself* has no *reality*.

This point is similar to the second question: If the self is unreal, aren't its thoughts also unreal?

To say that the self is unreal is to say that the self does not exist in actuality; therefore, of course, the self's thoughts do not actually exist.

But to raise a question about the "self" and its "thoughts" is to raise a question about "real" forms.

Such questions are empty of significance because any such questionable forms are empty of *reality* at the time the question is raised.

When we recognize that all forms are empty from the start—*including* the recognizer—what question of emptiness can possibly be asked?

The Grand Illusion

Clearly, since not anything truly exists, nothing really matters; therefore we need not "make too much" of ajata.

What ajata "adds on", to our recognition of nonduality, is that *advaita* can be seen to be another (empty) concept in a universe that is itself illusory. This is not to say that Self-realization has no freeing virtue, which it does, but *within* the overall illusion.

As you state, "The entire apparent Universe is," from the viewpoint of ajata, "uncreated and doesn't exist." Therefore, "I do accept that everything I 'experience' never has existed and is," therefore, "truly Empty." Self-realization, or nonduality through advaita, is one of the things we 'experience' in a universe that is uncreated.

You write, "'waking up' in the 'real world' is what we refer to as our death." And it can be viewed in two elaborations.

When we wake up that *all* is empty, that *is* our conse-quent death. But even if one thinks that "he" dies, in actuality, the grand *illusion* nevertheless *ends* with "his death."

The recognition (I call waking up within the Dream) that the universe, and all in it, has no everlasting reality frees us from all that is within the universe, immaterial concepts included.

We need cling to nothing, because that's all there ultimately is, anyway. We need not, beyond that, even question anything.

Unreal Phenomena

You quote Lamrimpa as saying that according to Nagar-juna, "for whom emptiness is possible, all phenomena are possible." What does this mean?

Phenomena are what we suppose are real, within the Dream world. However, one who has awakened from the Dream world knows that it is false. Therefore, any phenomena appearing to exist or be real within the Dream world are false or unreal.

For example, phenomena that are said to occur include miracles. Another phenomenon believed to occur are the laws of physics. Miracles and the laws of physics are contradictory. How can both be real? In fact, *both* are unreal.

It is because they are unreal that both can exist at the supposed same time, in the same place.

This is why, for Madhyamika, not anything needs to be disputed. Knowing that all things are empty of reality from the start, one unreality within the Dream is equal to any other unreality within the Dream. For whom emptiness is possible, *any* thing is possible. Put another way, anything is possible that is unreal anyway.

Q: To see this is a huge step, a profound shift in perspective…

K: When you see that nothing has ever happened, there are no more 'steps'.

Q: Then why are there 6 billion people who think that they and the world exist?

K: It's the other way around: As long as you think you exist, there are 6 billion people.

Karl Renz

How To

Can you say what it is that "brings us into" the Dream?

The question of importance is: What *keeps* us in the Dream? The answer is: We start from an unquestioned assumption that we "live" in a universe which is real; and that as a presumed observer of these things, "I" am equally real.

How do we "wake up from" the Dream? To discover (for instance, through advaita) that "I" do not actually exist, it can be understood that an unreal me is proposing an assumption that the universe which "I" observe is nevertheless—without question—real. Mutually, a self-substantiating conclusion.

Since the conclusion is that anything in this Dream—e.g., its universe and I—is actually existent, it is the source of our inevitable suffering (such as fear of death). As Buddha eloquently made clear, the key to *waking up* is the realization of the inherent emptiness of the "self". For example:

> Sariputra (a disciple), when a wise being practices the perfection of wisdom, he does not see a ('person') as real.... A person is empty of being an inherently-existent being.

Last night's dream and yesterday's life are the same. Both are gone. Both were illusions. It is true, just as the wisdom masters have told us, that life is a dream. Some images hold more meaning than others, but they have no greater substance...

I could not wait to be of more help to transitory dream people who suffer because they do not know that they are in a dream, and do not know that liberation is waking up to the dream as a dream.

Yongey Mingyur Rinpoche

The Big Question

Tad:

To answer your question: from the standpoint of ultimate reality, it doesn't matter what you say, feel, think or do: "you" are not the doer, as the advaita teachings say, because you do not exist as you think you are — a separate individual.

So, does it matter if you save a (separate) "life"?: no; as there is no you who has a life (as Buddha says in the Diamond Sutra), there are no lives, separate or otherwise.

The most refined, or deepest, investigation of advaita is known as ajata. Ajata teaches (as do I, at my website ajatasunyata.com) that our so-called reality is an illusion. We are dreamers, living in a dream: the dream has no reality, in any ultimate sense. We ourselves are *within* the dream; we are no more real than the dream itself. In other words, not any thing which occurs in this "universe" or "world"—good, bad, or neutral—is actually real, or true. So, does it *really* make any difference what we do? No: no more so than any difference it makes as to what is done in a *sleeping* dream.

In the big Dream, which occurs while we're awake (in particular), we are conditioned to presuppose that certain things "exist", in addition to our selves: such as time, space and cause-and-effect, even life or death.

As dreamers within the Dream, these things which we are conditioned to believe exist—such as, for instance, "I" or "death"—shape the nature of our Dream. As a dreamer, "I" will suppose, for instance, that "life" (especially mine) has a higher value than "death" (especially mine). Therefore, one will consider it most sensible to "save lives". But not anything which occurs in the dream has any actual reality.

So, to answer your question, in the Dream you will, or you will not, attempt to save someone's life. Apart from (or "outside" of) the unreal Dream, it makes no difference what you do, or do not do. Not any thing within the Dream has any reality, from an ultimate standpoint.

As the Buddhists point out, every thing within the illusion which we call life, and this universe, is "empty of reality". Likewise, anything beyond (or "apart" from) this illusive life and universe is equally "empty of reality". *Ultimate* reality is "emptiness" (Sanskrit: sunyata).

In *emptiness*, not anything matters. In fact, in emptiness not anything has ever actually happened or occurred. Why? Because from emptiness, not anything can actually ever have originated or "arisen". This tells us *why* "life" is a dream of an unreal dreamer within the unreal Dream.

Empty from the Start

The deepest spiritual truth is one in which the arising of questions becomes impossible when it is realized. Once one has this answer, all else is self-revealing. This answer, in a sentence, the sages tell us, is that not anything has ever been created or originated from the very outset. For one, Hui Neng, the sixth Chinese patriarch, has said: "Since there is nothing from the start, how can dust [also meaning ignorance, in Buddhism] alight?"

Where there is not any thing from the start, the condition would be emptiness. From total emptiness, there is not any thing which can arise. Where not any thing arises, there can only be emptiness. Emptiness and no creation are the same, and mean that not anything exists or has reality (or non-reality).

So anything which it is thought has been created or exists, or has reality, is not so (and this includes thoughts as well).

If there was anything which *had* actually arisen, from a condition of emptiness, it could not have been arisen by way of emptiness: it would have to be self-originating. Being self-caused, it would be *independent* of reliance on cause. Being independent of cause, it would as well be independent of effect. In other words, it would never effect (or be effected by) the forces of change, of birth, aging or death. Not anything that we know of, that appears to us in this world, fits this description.

This description can fit only emptiness itself—which is the only condition that has ever been present.

And from that condition of emptiness, not anything has ever happened, in actuality, because not anything has ever actually existed in reality.

Sunyata: Emptiness

In his later years, Buddha was a teacher of sunyata: form is emptiness, emptiness is form. Because of the difficulty for the followers to understand the subject, it is said, he normally did not delve deeply into it. An exception, perhaps would be the discourse to a particular follower that he gave in Sri Lanka, known as the Lankavatara Sutra.

Around the Second Century A.D., an Indian monk wrote a poetic treatise in which—using logic that any philosopher would admire—he set out proofs of Buddha's thesis.

While emptiness is more difficult to comprehend, we all know what *forms* are: we view *ourselves* as forms. So, Nagarjuna's explanations concern "dependent arising", or co-arising. Any thing which is dependent upon something else, whatever it is, for its existence—and that means *every thing*—does not exist on its own or by its own right. Therefore, being empty of autonomy, it is empty of true existence. What does not really exist cannot be claimed to be truly real.

So while things appear to be existent and real, they cannot actually be: all such appearances are empty of reality. In other words, the true nature of forms is their incontrovertible emptiness: "form is emptiness".

Although, by taking on the subject of form first, one has an obvious and comprehensible way to engage emptiness, this traditional explanation has its limits. Buddha also taught that there is "no arising".

What this means is that if something arises—is created, or originated (that is, comes into form)—the arising would be an effect for which there would have to be a cause.

Where the original condition was one of no arising, it would be a purely empty condition: not anything can arise from complete emptiness.

Therefore, to begin a discussion of emptiness on the basis of co-arising is to essentially *create* the forms which are said to co-arise—and which need to be seen as not real and not truly existing in the final analysis of emptiness. No forms can ever have been formed in a condition in which there is no arising.

Emptiness is a cause-less condition. Yet any thing which exists will have been caused. And all things, therefore, would be dependent upon causations, if nothing else. Causation is behind the idea of dependent *arising*.

The obvious end to the limitation of presenting form first, and its dependent arising, is to initially emphasize the condition of *no* arising—from which not anything has ever actually been created or originated in the first place.

Thus one can appreciate the genius of Hui Neng's lines ("dust" is a Buddhist metaphor for ignorance):

> When there is nothing from the start,
> Where can dust alight?

No Arising

Ajata is the consequential condition in understanding emptiness: ajata means, in Sanskrit, "no creation".

A theoretical objector to emptiness says to Nagarjuna:

> "If all this were void, then there would be *no creation*, and no destruction." Nagarjuna says, "If all this is *empty*, then there *is* no arising and no disintegrating."

When we say the universe is empty, we do not mean that the universe is empty of everything except for the indiscernible Absolute (as nonduality teaches). The Absolute, as a cognizable thing, is itself *within* the Dream, as is even the very *idea* of it. The universe (being unreal) is empty of the reality, or existence, of every "thing"; *including* the Absolute.

Paul Williams:

> In other words, if we think of ultimate reality as an Absolute, the really inherently Real, the Madhyamaka claim is that there is no such thing. *There is no Absolute.*

Harsh Narain:

> Nagarjuna's suggestion is that his denial of the world does not imply belief in another order of reality like the Absolute, immanent in or transcendent to phenomena.

Being is positive reality and *no* being is negative reality, and the Madhyamika will not recognize any reality whatsoever, positive or negative, much less the Absolute.

D.T. Suzuki:

The first declaration made by Hui-neng regarding his Zen experience was that 'From the first not a thing is', and then he went on to the 'Seeing into one's self-nature', which self-nature, being 'not a thing', is nothingness....

Hui-neng's whole mission was to break down this barrier; hence his statement: 'From the first not a thing is.' This must have troubled his disciples ever since it came out of the mouth of a supposedly ignorant wood-cutter of Shinchou.

Nargarjuna's definitive statement:

No things whatsoever exist, at any time, in any place, having arisen of themselves, from another, from both or without cause....

From things that are but empty,

Empty things arise and that is all!

David Godman said of Ramana, "his own experience was that creation itself had never occurred, except in the imagination."

In his *Authentic Portrait of the Middle Way*, Milarepa sang:

The true nature of appearances is that they've never been *born*....
All animate, inanimate—
Unborn and nonexistent from the outset,
No base to rest on.

Lucretius:

Nothing can come from nothing.

Stephen Batchelor:

> It is realized not by denying anything existent,
> but by negating something that has never existed
> at all.

Michael James stresses that not only the "real" but the "unreal" haven't seen creation:

> The ultimate truth is that no illusory appearance
> has ever come into *existence*...

B. Alan Wallace adds, "if something is not produced, it does not depart from non-existence."

Chandrakirti:

> Therefore, "production" is always non-existent.
> Since there is no production, forms and so forth
> do not exist.... Phenomena's true nature itself
> has no essence — this is the "emptiness of the
> true nature." It is called "true nature" because no
> one created it.... There is not even 'nonarising' as
> such. Because arising things do not exist.

Khenpo Tsultrim Gyamtso:

> What then is the nature of the "arising" that we
> see happening in the world all the time? It is mere
> appearance, just like the arising that appears to
> happen in dreams. As long as we dream and do
> not know that we are dreaming, we believe that
> the arising we see happening in the dream is real.
> As soon as we recognize that we are dreaming,
> however, we know that the arising is just a mere
> appearance that has no reality to it at all.

Crosby and Skilton:

> Something *eternal* has no beginning and so can-
> not have been created.

And what is eternal? Emptiness. Emptiness itself is not some thing to which "beginning" or "ending" would apply in its description.

Where not anything has ever been created, from the beginning, the *idea* of causation and its effects is another element within the universal Dream.

The Dream, as with the unreal thought process itself, is a consequence of an endless chain of cause and effect. It is not real.

Physicist Stephen Hawking:

> You can't get to a time before the Big Bang because there was no time before the Big Bang. We have finally found something that doesn't have a cause, because there was no *time* for a cause to exist *in*.

Causation itself is not real. Tsultrim:

> There is nothing that *can* arise; there is no event of arising at all that can occur without the presence of causes and conditions to make it happen. Furthermore, whatever arises in *dependence* upon causes and conditions does not truly arise.

Shantideva:

> If something truly *exists*, what does it need with a cause? Moreover, if something is non-existent, what does *it* need with a cause?

B. Alan Wallace:

> Prevailing interpretations of quantum mechanics emphasize the lack of strict causality in the quantum world... The notion that the universe, and

all the sentient beings who dwell in it, have no ultimate beginning is often hard to grasp by the Western mind.... However, in stating that entities are produced, if one means that they exist not simply by the power of convention, but by their *own* power, they would exist independently, without reliance upon other conditions. If something existed in that way, it would have no need for a cause, for it would already *exist* by its own power.

Think about it. How could the *universe* have been caused, when causation has to be an *effect* of the "creation" (caused) of the universe?

This realization is the sudden end-result of the conviction, the constantly (mentally) repeated irresistible refrain, "It does not matter—nothing matters."

That is the final conclusion you come to! Nothing really matters.

Ramesh Balsekar

Emptiness: Nothing *Really* Matters

The view of "no origin" (or, no origination) is simple: not any thing has started from a beginning, at any time, anywhere. "No origin" means there has not been an origin—or beginning—of *beginnings* (or of time either, for that matter; or even a "where").

With not anything ever originated, or "created", this does not mean that the universe has somehow always existed as it is. "No origination" means that a universe itself has not come into existence.

In other words, the view of "no origination" says that the universe itself cannot be a real existence. The mistaken beings who claim that the universe, and its worlds, do exist as such, are themselves unreal because there can have been no creation of *forms*, whether material (like humans) or immaterial (like ideas or thoughts).

So, the emptiness implied by no origination does not suggest a universe or cosmos which is empty of all things, it is saying there has not been a *universe* from the start.

A difficulty a human has of perceiving this view point is apparently in "his" capacity to conclude that what he has *sensed*—seen, heard, etc.—is existent and therefore *real* (or real and therefore existent). The eyes look down and notice the human form and the brain supposes that "I am here, I exist, I am real". The eyes look up at something seemingly apart from "me"—a world—and the brain cognizes that this too is there and exists as real.

As long as our supposition is that "I"—or anything other than I—have existence, we are starting from the presumptive bias that there is indeed some *thing*.

From the point of view that there is in reality *no thing* whatsoever, it would be contradictory to approach the proposition of no origination by holding on to the reservation that any—even one: me—-thing resides *outside* of that proposition of "no creation".

No creation also means no creatures. "You", as creature, cannot stand outside or apart from the proposition of no creation and attempt to make sense of it.

So, it is not a legitimate question to ask "If there is nothing from the start, how am I here?" The teachings are telling you that your human *understanding* of reality and the *truth* of (so-called) reality are not the same. And these teachings are telling you much more that has an effect on "your life".

Leading in toward the understanding of no creation, or emptiness, is advaita: the word itself, in Sanskrit, means "not two"; no two (or more) things exist — including "me" or "other than me".

The foremost exponent of advaita in our time was Ramana Maharshi, who pointed his enlightened disciples toward ajata, which in Sanskrit means no creation, or no origination.

Ramana, though, focused his attention on first bringing his disciples to enlightenment, by showing that the underlying nature of all relative forms must be the formless Absolute. Advaita states that all that is, is the Absolute. According to ajata, or no origination, there cannot *even* be the Absolute.

Ramana has stated his fundamental teaching is ajata (though his remarks are mostly directed to those who have yet to comprehend advaita).

His position:

> There is no creation, in the state of Realization.... Only if there is creation do we have to explain how it came about... There is no alternative but to accept the world as unreal, if you are seeking the Truth and the Truth alone.

H.W.L. Poonja, or "Papaji", had his awakening through Ramana, and also became a teacher of advaita. As with Ramana, his deeper seeing was into ajata.

He said:

> You have never allowed yourself to experience the emptiness that is empty of all objects.... What is seen does not exist.... No one exists; nothing exists... Because I know the truth that nothing has ever happened... what need was there for a creation at all?... One can say this with authority only when one abides in that ultimate place where nothing has ever happened.

Early ajata writings were accredited to Guadapada, the predecessor to Shankara's teacher. As with all Indian sages, including Buddha, Guadapada was conversant with the Vedic gitas. The Ashtavakra Gita, for example (excerpts):

> All this is the product of illusion, and nothing exists as "objects" in an undivided reality.

The "universe" itself is a figment of imagination.
The universe, even though it seems present to the
senses, is unreal.

With the calming of the wind of the mind creating forms, the universe meets destruction (as a
defined object).

The universe does not in reality exist.

This manifold universe is nothing... nothing
exists.

What came through Guadapada as ajata was ostensi-
bly the Madhyamaka (or, Madhyamika) school of the
Buddha's deepest teachings, which are given primarily
in two major sutras.

In the Heart Sutra, an awakened disciple is speaking to a
senior disciple, in Buddha's presence:

"Form is emptiness, emptiness is form.... all
phenomena are emptiness... in emptiness there
is no form... no consciousness... no mind... no
mental objects (thoughts, concepts, perceptions
etc.)... (nor an) origin."

Hearing this, Buddha exclaimed: "Excellent!... It is just
so... Just as you have revealed".

The Dalai Lama has commented on the Heart Sutra:

As one's understanding of the ultimate nature of
reality deepens, one begins to recognize more
clearly the erroneous nature of one's belief in
intrinsic existence. If one understands emptiness... there is simply no basis for grasping onto
selfhood to arise. From this practical perspective... emptiness constitutes the highest and most
subtle understanding of the Buddha's teaching on
no-self... Even the resultant state of clarity that
arises from clear penetration into the perfection

of wisdom is itself empty of intrinsic existence. Finally, and this is a crucial point, even emptiness itself is devoid of intrinsic existence... emptiness is therefore both the means of eliminating the mental afflictions and the resultant state that one arrives at after having done so.

In the Diamond Sutra, Buddha addresses a disciple. Buddha states that those who...

...gain perfect clarity of mind... do not create the perception of a *self*. Nor do they create the perception of a *being*, a *life*.... Nor do thoughts really exist. Subhuti, a past thought cannot be found. A future though cannot be found. Nor can a present thought be found.

He advised that each discover "the self-less, birthless nature" of reality; renounce "self existence every day". He emphasizes, "No beginning [and thus no finite ending], Subhuti, is the highest truth."

"Subhuti," said Buddha, "undifferentiated is this dharma in which nothing (no thing) is differentiated." No "this" or "that". And, he said, as "an illusion...a bubble, a dream....view all 'created' things like this."

Where there is no self, there is no thinker who creates differentiated perceptions, or thoughts. Where there is no such thing as a self, there is no self which perceives a "world". All conceived forms have a beginning and an ending, as contrasted with emptiness.

The sixth Chinese patriarch, Hui Neng, said that he came to enlightenment through overhearing a recitation of the Diamond Sutra. Later the Zen master delivered a commentary on this sutra.

Hui Neng received his appointment as a roshi by winning a poetry contest designed to show the depth of the aspirants' realization. The last two lines of his short poem are a summary of emptiness.

> There being nothing, from the start,
> Where can dust alight?

Dust also can mean, in Buddhism, confusion. The point of ajata/madhyamaka is that where we have surmised that not anything has ever actually been real, or existed, from the start, where can our problems, confusions, or suffering appear from? Clearly, if there was not a single mind in the universe, could it be said that a universe *existed*? When we perceive that thoughts, phenomenon, selves, time, place, etc., are all dependent on discriminations in the human mind which supposes their reality, how can any of these "manifestations" be taken seriously enough to invite reactions?

When Ramana says, "nothing in fact ever happens", what in *that* case "really matters" in an ultimate sense?

Buddha said treat this life as "an illusion... a dream". Not anything, in a dream, really *matters*!

What Matters

The universe does not exist in reality because causality, "creation", does not exist in reality. "You" are in the "universe"; there being no universe, in reality, what difference does it make what anyone does (or does not do) in this world?

Here's how Zen master Takuan advised samurai Munenori:

> The uplifted sword has no will of its own, it is all of emptiness. The man who is about to be struck down is also of emptiness, and so is the one who wields the sword. None of them are possessed of a mind which has any substantiality. As each of them is of emptiness and has no "mind", the striking man is not a man, the sword in his hands is not a sword, and the "I" who is about to be struck down is like the splitting of the spring breeze in a flash of lightning. (Of no ultimate consequence.)

Fletcher and Blankleder:

> Good and evil, and all the conventions of ordinary life, are utterly negated and without significance.

Tsultrim:

> If we are not able to reverse this tendency to think that right and wrong are truly existent, it will be impossible for us to realize emptiness.

In emptiness, there is not anything; there is not any thing that moves, there is no activity. Because in reality there has never been anything from the start, not any thing has ever actually "happened".

Nagarjuna:

> On the path that has been traveled, there is no moving,
>
> On the path that has not been traveled, there is no moving either.

Garma Chang:

> Emptiness implies motionlessness... like the Void, it is always at rest, rising above the processes of construction and destruction.
>
> Emptiness implies the positive negation... it negates all that which has limits or ends.

Ramana Maharshi:

> Whatever you see happening in the waking state happens only to the knower, and since the knower is unreal, nothing in fact ever happens.

Tsultrim:

> However, in order to understand the true nature of reality, we must realize that nothing ever really happens. We must realize that arising and birth are not real. Therefore, Nagarjuna analyzes causes, conditions, and arising, and he proves that they are in fact empty of any inherent nature... and since none of them are valid, things do not truly arise. Therefore, things do not truly exist.

In the *Prajnaparamita Sutras*, the Buddha taught:

> No beginning is perceptible,

No end is perceptible,
And nothing in between is perceptible either.

Dalai Lama:

Therefore, all consciousnesses are mistaken except for the wisdom that directly cognizes emptiness.

Frederick Streng:

The apprehension of emptiness is a solution to all problems, not because "a solution" has been found, but because the problems have ceased to be "problems".

Longchenpa:

It is of no concern whether or not all thoughts and expressions are transcended.

It is of no concern whether or not confused attempts at proof and refutation are demolished.

It is of no concern whether or not the view to be realized has been realized.

Conclusion:

A Tendai abbot stepped forward with a tray and declared, "This tray contains the universe." Daito smashed the tray with his stick—"What happens when the universe is crushed?"

What matters, where the ultimate condition is empty of reality?

Not anything really matters!

When I attained Absolute Perfect Enlightenment, I attained absolutely nothing.

Buddha

Made in United States
North Haven, CT
20 January 2023

31278616R00065